Kusano Shinpei is one of Japan's most distinguished and surprising modern poets. Mt Fuji, holy mountain that since at least the 8th century has been seen as symbolic of Japan itself, was one of his most enduring facinations. Virtually all of the Mt. Fuji poems are translated into English here for the first time.

> *... thoughtful and careful and close versions of Shinpei-san's marvelous Fuji poems.*
>   Cid Corman

Japanese names are given in the traditional order, family name first.

Asian Poetry in Translation: Japan
Editor, Thomas Fitzsimmons

#1 *Devil's Wind: A Thousand Steps* by Yoshimasu Gozo

#2 *Sun, Sand and Wind* by Shozu Ben

#3 *A String Around Autumn: Selected Poems 1952-1980* by Ooka Makoto

#4 *Treelike: The Poetry of Kinoshita Yuji*
  -- Japan-US Friendship Commission Translation Prize

#5 *Dead Languages: Selected Poems 1946-1984* by Tamura Ryuichi

#6 *Celebration in Darkness: Selected Poems of Yoshioka Minoru*
  &
  Strangers' Sky: Selected Poems of Iijima Koichi

#7 *A Play of Mirrors: Eight Major Poets of Modern Japan*

#8 *A Thousand Steps . . . and More: Selected Poems and Prose 1964-1984* by Yoshimasu Gozo

#9 *Demented Flute: Selected Poems 1967-1986* by Sasaki Mikiro

#10 *I Am Alive: The Tanka Poems* of Goto Miyoko

#11 *Moonstone Woman: Selected Poems and Prose* by Tada Chimako

#12 *Self-Righting Lamp: Selected Poems* by Maruyama Kaoru

#13 *Mt. Fuji: Selected Poems 1943-1986* by Kusano Shinpei

Supported by the National Endowment for the Arts, the Japan-US Friendship Commission, Oakland University (MI), University of Michigan Center for Japanese Studies, the Saison Cultural Foundation (Japan), the University of Sydney (Australia) and UNESCO.

Mt Fuji
Selected Poems 1943-1986

Asian Poetry in Translation : Japan #13

Mt Fuji
Selected Poems 1943-1986

Kusano Shinpei

Translated by

Leith Morton

Introduction by Cid Corman

Katydid Books
Oakland University   Michigan

Copyright © 1991 by Katydid Books
English translations Copyright © 1991 by Leith Morton
Introduction Copyright © 1991 by Cid Corman
Cover art Copyright © 1991 by Karen Hargreaves-Fitzsimmons

All rights reserved

First Edition

Produced by KT DID Productions, Inc
Printed in the United States of America
by Thomson-Shore, Dexter, MI

Published with the aid of a grant from the University of Sydney, Australia.

This book is printed on acid-free paper and its binding materials have been chosen for strength and durability.

KATYDID BOOKS:
K.H.-Fitzsimmons and T. Fitzsimmons, assisted by G.L. Robinson
c/o Department of English, Oakland University, Rochester, MI 48309-4401
FAX 313-370-2286

Distributed by University of Hawaii Press, Honolulu, HI 96822

Library of Congress Cataloging in Publication Data

Kusano, Shinpei, 1903-1988
    Mt. Fuji, selected poems 1943-1986 / Kusano Shinpei ; translated by Leith Morton ; introduction by Cid Corman.
        p. cm. - - (Asian poetry in translation. Japan ; 13)
    Translation from various Japanese books.
    ISBN 0-942668-30-8. - - ISBN 0-942668-29-4 (pbk.)
    1. Kusano, Shinpei, 1903-   - -Translations, English.   I. Corman, Cid. II. Title. III. Title: Mount Fuji, selected poems 1943-1986. IV. Series.
PL832.U75A27   1991
895.6'15- -dc20   91-2255
                                            CIP

Contents

Introduction
    Cid Corman 11

The Poems 15

Translator's Afterword 89

Notes 92

A dot (·) after the final line on a page signifies a stanza break.

Introduction

Cid Corman

It would only be adding lustre to lustre to speak of Leith's thoughtful and careful and close versions of Shinpei-san's marvellous Fuji poems.
 There are recordings of the man reading his own work and one day when people learn to listen to poetry again — that fine voice of his will be heard and all those seemingly inarticulate syllables start to speak to us and through us again.
 Perhaps it is not inapt to cite my own words published in REKITEI (the magazine to which he contributed so much) as a memorial. (Leith was with me at the service referred to.)
:
There are so few human beings. Most of us at most pretend to be one of them once in a while. When the fact of being breaks in upon and over us enough to be the act of being — of being more than ourselves (as George Oppen said).
 Shinpei-san — the first moment we (Kamaike-san and I) were with him — his last day in the hospital — winter of 1965 — showed us the whiskey parked under his pillow with a smile (he drank too much but...), put on bathrobe and slippers and led us out to where we could share a few beers and be together.
 It was like him to be himself.
 Poverty — he clearly knew from the start — was the source of poetry. And he was giftedly poor. Poverty is the compassionate lamp of the truth's imagination.
 There are those who think poetry is a form of idleness or a pleasant hobby or a dilettante amusement or a strait way to fame (few of us wear spurs these days — or hair shirts for that matter). Shinpei-san knew — in the midst of his life — poetry is the life itself as the life itself. A terrible redundancy. The way breath will repeat itself. What we cant swallow or have enough of.
 His poetry then — as now — begins at the constant beginning — word of breath — at the mouth — drawn from heart/mind/spirit. At the simple depth of unwearying lucidity. Earth, body, breath, pain, and the other for whom the echo is home. Frog fish dog dinosaur — star sun moon ocean sky Fuji — friends food flowers festivals.
 Where does the word end? You open a book as you open your hand to a fortune teller. There are just those lines to be read — the matter to be told.

12 — KUSANO SHINPEI

I said it at his memorial service and I say it again: Shinpei-san — you are never less than present. You have never been less than here — nearer than near. It has nothing to do with being Japanese — whatever that means — or even being a man — whatever that means — but only and always with being — as you always were and always will be — alive — alive alive O! And how your poetry knows it!

Glows it. Glozes it.

"a single eye,

sharp ear.

Somewhere.
spring thunder's.
presentiment.

Your birth day begins again.

THE FROG MAN

He could hardly see
or hear or speak or
stand — let alone eat —

and yet in his room
in the company
of poetry he

eked out voice to sing
in languages the
exact word of what •

any word must mean:
we come back to this
being together.

Cid Corman
22 May 1989 — 17 Feb. 1990

1943

I dedicate these poems to the future of Japan

I
At the mountain base peaches, cherries, apricots blossom.
Among massing flowers butterflies dance.
Millions & millions of butterflies dance.
Rainbow coloured mist rises.

My dreaming.
Fuji festival.

All around flowers bloom.
All around butterflies dance.
All the ancient instruments begin to play.
Like at seed-time, birds gather.
All the birds in Japan gather.
Singing with the instruments.

My dreaming.
Fuji festival.

Rainbow coloured mist is lit by the snow.
Turns to rainbow coloured heat-haze, shimmers.
Deer, wild boar, bears, horses.
No people? They're here, they're here!
Gourd *saké* and a woman's dance.
The men of the sacred grove, they too, are singing.

Ah.
My dreaming.
Fuji festival.•

From its distant snow-covered ridges golden orioles.
Become envoys, flowers in their beaks, crossing.
Crossing back three oceans.

II
Utterly.
Ash-grey, the colour of snow.
The single colour, ash-grey, falling falling falling becomes, unnoticed, a huge wave.
A bellow without direction, not south, not north.
Above a sea of trees the snow erupts into spray.
Joining a new ash-grey huddle.
Blown together, blown apart, spearing into a great snow wall.
Collapsing, sinking.
A raging ash cloud climbing.

>Is it this? The feast offered.
>By the gods to the love they so envy.
>Between the vast emptiness of the dome of heaven.
>And the harsh, iridescent mountain peak.

From where do they continue to roll? Millions & millions of.
Waves of blizzards and mountain peaks.
Piercing like wire, the screams of Asura.

>Ah, in its bowels.
>Does it reach the depths of heaven? *Fuji-basalt* sleeps silently.

III
From the beginning of time.
Hundreds of millions of days and black nights.
A great body sitting heavily within the vast vacuum of time.

>Ah.
>From confrontation after confrontation.

Though it be only a tiny gesture, I sang small songs.
And yet far far away from my praise.

Far far away.
A soaring harmonic.
An inexhaustible body.
A fierce, great white spirit.

IV
Spring sunlight spills fire over the surface of the river.
A breeze springs up and light plays, reeds murmur. Reed
warblers call. On their tongues too spring sunlight.

On the clover field beneath the bank.
My face in my two hands.
I gazed, somehow weary.
In a flood of spring sunlight.

Girls pluck the clover blossoms and deftly weave flower-garlands.
These they use as ropes to jump with. A circle of flower-
garlands appears, into it jumps Fuji. Each turn Fuji draws
closer. Then recedes far away.

In my ears reed warblers.
On my cheeks sunlight.

V
Fire mountain
Flames glittering red on the snow.
On the snow-shoulder peaceful flames glittering.
Flaring silently into the night.
In the bowels of night dying.
Ah, above.
In the moon vastness directly above.

Great coils looping, a blue rope.

   I want to approach.
   To question the dragon.

Life's joys life's sorrows, as if all that equals nothing.
Not wreathed in its usual cloud spiral.
On its gilt-beguiling scales flames glittering.
Lu-la lu-la-la
Sharp eyes closing, sharp talons sheathing.
Lu-la lu-la-la looping.

VI
A piece of the heavy dark cloud moves suddenly. It mushrooms.
Mushrooming mushrooming spiralling up like an electric corkscrew
in an instant to the heavens. Cloud spirals loops-the-loop.
In the lonely dark dusk spiralling spearing through the thick
cloud-mass to the heavens above No. 1 mountain. <Ah. The
same old road. The same old loop the same old mess of cloud.>
Out of a violent, bitter dread. Flexing scales drenched
by the sea, it rose straight as an arrow. Bzzbzzbzzbzz that's
the lash of its thick wiry vibrissa. Frenzied cloud colliding
disintegrating makes its torso trochilics of 6 & 8. Empty
talons tearing at the wind. Burning eyes penetrate the darkness.
Beyond turn & twist & trochilics. From a forever eternal sight.
Ecstatic thundering blows it the cloud away.

As far as the far-off horizon the sea is calm.
Inside the cave against which the tide breaks.
Silence.

In a perfectly clear orange sky.
The black massive.
Roof of Japan.

VII
Partnering planet earth.
Diving through the night.
Ah.
First of all, Nippon.
Rose peak.

VIII
Leaf sea settles cloud sea settles inside the clouds.
Fuji settles.

IX
Silver grasslands hold their breath.
Demon's mirror, the moon.
Is brilliant.

X
Japan's symbol.
Even at night doesn't sleep.

XI
Like drops fallen from heaven.
These bird's eye petal-crowns, why is one so partially
white? Why are three of the crowns blue? And why is one
of the three so dark?
On the steps along the path I walk each day. How can
they keep blossoming for so many months?
I wonder to myself.
Evening dew glitters in a *saké* cup 6 millimetres in diameter.
By sipping my lips may grow sweet.
Even the paraffin-like cloud opposite I prefer.
To lovely still nature.

Feeling as if I want to raise in opposition the roar of a
wild beast I climb the steps.
At the top a great embankment.
So bold so bare Fuji I yearn to embrace.

XII
At the limits of the sea.
Fuji calls to far K'un-lun.
At the limits of the sea.
K'un-lun responds to our far-off Fuji.

XIII
Devil's island.
Travelling far from even the Koch'a islands.
The sea of crude oil is heavy and tepid.
Without waves, heavy and tepid.
The heavens are ultramarine.
Opening wide.

    Good-bye.
    Good-bye.

Ah.
From the sea of crude oil.
Fuji rising.

On the Koch'a islands.
The humpbacked rock can no longer be seen.
The heavens are ultramarine.
Overwhelming the eye.

    Good-bye.
    Good-bye.•

Pressing closer.
(Nippon)
Fuji rising.

XIV
Look!
There's Fuji.

Ai Yah!
Pointing at the mountain vaster lovelier than I had dreamed of.

Long long suppressed my tears.
Ran.

XV
Morning after the ruthless screaming blizzard.
The line between ultramarine and white stinging.
Ah.
Utterly translucent great peak.

In the north attended by tusk-like jagged Alps.
On and on the mountain slope.
Descending into the frothy sea distant and deep continuing
on to the island-specks of Micronesia.

   Deep within the vastness of night.
   Dyeing the snow red.
   An inflamed sky.
   <781 A.D. 782 A.D.>
      Sometimes Fuji tore apart and flowed into heaven.

      Now *Fuji-basalt* sleeps silently.
      <Jets birds flash back and forth through the blue>•

Big beautiful peace.
Soars aloft in song.

Ah but that peak translucent in all aspects.
Pressed by fire from the earth-axis.
May yet ram heaven.

XVI
Breeze
A breeze blows & instead it turns hot.
Rain dissolved mid-stream into steam & once more went back
to the orange heaven.

Beyond the black tangle of fern clusters.
A thousand miles of mud.
Dinosaurs clashed spraying gobbets of mud.

The sea revealed no horizon.
Morning dawned.
Night fell.
On the mist & forest scroll of the Japanese archipelago.
One day silent flames rose.
On top of the mountain mountains of molten mud grew.

And often
Scorched the leaden snowy heavens.

Sucking sun.
Sucking water.
Warring against the wind.

Deep within the vast star-furred firmament.
Eternal (Fuji).
Merciful (Fuji).
Inexhaustible (Fuji).

A thousand centuries old Fuji has come to be what it is now.

The vast temple of the leafsea.
Is a free hotel.
For birds.
The bare brilliant mountain mass.
Is free spiritual nourishment.
For the people.

Moon & blade & rush-hat.
Many-petaled love & aeroplanes.
& history drift.
Embracing the <world> Fuji scowls silently.

Dinosaurs are napping.
Shrouded in mist.
The sea revealed no horizon.

Ah now.
After fire & storm & sacrificial suicide
To the musical accompaniment of 170 species of birds, over 10,000 birds.

White beautiful peace.
Lifts into the dawn sky of Japan.

XVII
After thousands millions billions of years.
By the end of billions of years.
All life on earth may have died.
Trees grass birds frogs men.
Perhaps even moss & trepang.
Blue ice serrating cracking.
All will change that much.
Yet even after for a time Fuji squats stark.
O terrible beauty! Unmatched even in the age of fire.

The spirit of the Japanese people.
There gathers freezes.
White flame.
Blows from the summit.
Heaven silently descends to see this faith.

To Matsukata Saburō in the mountains

1944

Mt Fuji
Through the viscera of the fire-born mountain.
Courses a network of blue veins.
Spouting into five lakes.

Fire flaring.
Amethyst-coloured summer Fuji.
Sacred snow flakes.
Billions of tonnes of snow rasping winter Fuji.
Swimming in the light, spring Fuji.
Gigantic ultramarine.
Soaring slashing through the glassy heavens autumn Fuji.

The seasons of 365 days.
Not resting even for a single day.
Countless blue veins course through the viscera of the fire-born mountain.
Spouting into five lakes.

Black Fuji
At the limit of Ushiku.
At the furthest limit of its mountain range.
Still higher than the mountain range.

Black Fuji.

Awesome.
Remote.
Black Fuji.

Cherry-red slowly darkens.
Up in the sky.

Gold-tinted.
Speck of cloud.

<Something infinite beyond existence.>
<Turning back to existence.>

Like prayer.

Remote.
Black Fuji.

1948

Volcano Fuji
Earthquake. I stretch & look.
From a window of a ramshackle inn.
Shocked. I race down. I look from the veranda's edge. From
the stone wall of the well & bucket in the garden.

>Forgive me.
>Everyone.
>I.
>At one extreme. In a miserable mood.
>Threw thunder & lightning at a quiescent Fuji.

>>Just as I imagined.
>>Just exactly as I imagined.
>>Mountain thunder: rumbling roaring seething sawing.
>>Eggplant purple.
>>Lifting.
>>Ah. Ah. Ah.
>>Lifting.
>>Lifting.

>Oh my wild design! It may be a vain & repellent fancy but.
>It signifies a rupture deep within my heart common to all
>at this moment in history, this hollow in history. A button
>I accidentally touched.

Once upon a time Fuji.
Squatted & scowled, fire mountain through all the four seasons.
And in truth no one knows when its seething interior might shoot up to heaven again.

>Dreamless, depressing.
>Superficial, obsequious, decadent.
>Hungry & corrupt.

A coreless.
Chaos: from an explosion of rage within me.

    Lifting.
    Lifting.
    Lifting.

The truth however.
What could it possibly symbolize?

    A giant blue litmus pillar of fire now.

My illusory reality vanishes.
3 a.m. in the darkness of my bed I.
Ask myself what in God's name are you?
Disconsolately open my eyes &
Shut them.

Cosmic Ray Fuji
Low low on the plain.
Locking in solid: a folding raincloud screen.

Right at the end.
Suddenly GHA.
Dusk fire.
Fuji.

Hurling pelting downwards.
Pale-indigo glass.
Huge squall.

1951

Firmament
Like a protruding navel.
Five centimetre Fuji.
The sea wherever you look blue tinplate.

> Gleaming so brightly that it turns dark.
> In the heavens black & purple grit grate out of tune.
> Waves of icy weather close upon the sun.
> SHASHASHASHASHAH ice clouds swim in the winds.

No people visible.
No birds no trees.

Like a protruding navel five centimetre Fuji.

Mt Fuji 1
Staining millions of cirrus fishing-lines.
Momentarily glowing.
Red-madder heaven.

Giant mortar.

> Muddied red in muddied river. On rusty iron on a roof on fire-debris muddied red like rusty iron. If this moment consuming heaven by flame staining the foreheads of the people on the ground were to cease suddenly. All would sink into heavy lead. In a pool of stagnant air somewhere white teeth snigger.

Binding solidly.
Sadness.
Giant mortar.•

Geography & history intersect. At their cross-shaped centre wildly aflame incandescent. No colour inside it what's sniggering? What's stuffed in the guts of a thing like that?

Even red-madder heaven.
Now pales.

Moving towards the giant mortar.
The gathering darkness.

Mt Fuji 2
Every day beauty is new in countless unknown flowers.
Old in obstinacy.
Silent in the vacuum of inanimate nature.

Masses of furry cloud lift silently in the night.
A bloody winter-cherry skates joyfully over the cloud-expanse.

Giant white porcelain.
Tinting eternity.
The pinkness of fresh-faced morning.

Mt Fuji 3
Ah.

Like a crimson beacon-fire.
Cloud-banners blaze & blaze.

Below.

> Hushed silence.
> A great golden being.

Drifting in the soft bright light countless.

Cloud-banners.

And below.

    Joined to the earth's axis.
    Golden.

From somewhere then welling up.
Music of the spheres.

Mt Fuji 4
Slashing.
Celadon-blurred heaven.
Beneath the rumble of the overhead J.N.R.* train. White geometry.

Over roof after roof.
Hard geometry.

Deep under roof after roof.
Seething molten magma.

Storing up rage.

Heaven shines.

**Japanese National Railways*

Mt Fuji Has a Big Laugh
On the afternoon of a day when I kept on thinking stupid thoughts.
Like I'd like to see Fuji speak one word.
In the language of human beings.

I heard.
On a tramline where you can't see Fuji.
A big crazy laugh.
Not an ordinary laugh a howl or a scolding.

Mt Fuji splitting its sides jawquaking.
That's what I thought I heard.
A hoarse guffaw like a shout.
& shivering came to a dead stop.
The tram was chock-a-block.
Squalid squashed filthy.
Chock-a-block: a symbol of the modern age.

Like the asthmatic hack of a whale or something.
Collapsed into throat-clearing.
Rolling onwards ever nearer that's what.
I heard.

1968

Break Fuji Break!
... 'The fissure in Mt Fuji in the last ten years has become much worse especially from about halfway to the summit. The recent changes in appearance of Mt Fuji have created quite a stir in the local area. In a meeting today Mr. Suzuki Tsuyoshi of the Socialist Party and Mr. Kodaira Yoshihei of the Kōmeitō Party took up the issue claiming that "the appearance of the sacred peak of Mt Fuji which has until now symbolized Japan will be ruined." They urged that countermeasures be taken by the local office of the Ministry of Construction. The Minister of Construction, Mr. Nishimura, stated in response that "If the fissure widens much more then no doubt difficulties will arise. I will commission an urgent study and work toward large-scale countermeasures...".' (25 May 1967 article in the local page of the Tokyo Asahi Newspaper)

Fuji is not a sacred mountain.
Fuji is a mountain.
Just a mountain.
Just a mountain but the symbolic existence of Japan.

3776 metre majestic cone. Companions include Myōkō. Yatsugatake. The Hakone range. Miharayama. Hachijō Fuji. The Fuji volcanic belt to the west of Niigata prefecture descends into the Sea of Japan and to the south extends from the seven islands of Izu to the Ogasawara chain. Diving again into the sea, bathed in sea snow, reaching to the Marianas an eerie dragon corpse.

The mountain moves.
To move is the mountain's destiny.
Massive example: the Ōsawa landslide.
2800 metres long. 500 metres wide. 125 metres deep. Landslide from summit to exact centre. Every day 50 tip-truck loads — 300 tonnes — of volcanic ash gravel and rock slide down.

Rain etc.
Wind etc.

Silent erosion.
The mountain diminishes.
To diminish is the mountain's destiny.
Gouging out itself movement is the mountain's destiny.

The mountain increases.
This too is the mountain's destiny.
November 1707.
In front of Fuji Edo darkened.
Musashi. Sagami. Suruga inconceivable how much ash.
Sudden bursting.
Columning up from the side.
On a cosmic scale.
Only yesterday.
It happened. In the time of the fifth Shōgun Tsunayoshi 260 years ago.
On the other side tomorrow the day after.
It may open.
A huge mouth.
(Though the earth is infirm the blood of youth still exists.)

Do our parliamentary representatives consider Fuji's fate?
Do they sense its terrible energy?
Day after day can they resist 50 tip-truck loads of landslide?
Day after day 50 tip-truck loads of concrete?
How many years.
Will it continue?
The lot who love to carp and prod.
Want to devise a plan of defence.
With this reply question time ended.
Why a defence is necessary was not discussed.
Why destiny should be denied was not discussed.
Bandai's V. If it ends like that.
Will 'the sacred peak of Fuji' disappear?
Will the beauty of 'the sacred peak of Fuji' disappear?
(Leave the sacred peak to pictures in public baths!)•

Parliamentary representatives of Japan. I myself know best. I am beyond your grasp, beyond your understanding. Stop your petty meddling! I'd rather you give up your miserly kindness. To break is my destiny. My strength. My beauty. To erupt is equally my destiny. My strength. My beauty. Do not use the valuable tax revenue of Japan on me. It will be blown away. Your Diet hang-out. If a mass of magma wells up beneath me. It's true. The bullet train Lake Hamana will burn & be buried beneath the ash. The eight Eastern provinces too will turn into a brilliant desert. I was particularly detached while I played a small game with the Ōsawa landslide. Give up this meaningless quarrelling. I will grow angry!

Fuji.
I want to see an even more terrible you.
Fuji. Breathe fire! In a V-shape.
Break Fuji break!
Expose your pudenda!

Today too Fuji for the First Time
To Hayashi Takeshi
19 March 1969 6:55 a.m. Akitsuppara.
Opposite.
Against alpine-rose dimly glowing.
White mortar.

Across the middle.
In a straight line.
Skylark dumdum explodes upward.
Now.
A cloudless sky.
Talking to itself.

Alpine-rose.

Winter Solstice
Into the centre of.
Fuji's peak.
Now a giant.
Sun sinks.
Now sinks.

Oh.
Seething.
Blood-stained heaven!

Growling at the raw smell.
of smoking barbecued lamb.

Celebrate the sun.
And the heavens!

<Right in the middle of an arid biting winter>

Blood-stained heaven!
Shine from a cup of cold *saké*!

Red Fuji
Powdered snow dancing madly.
Shining pink.
<mosquito-net melee>
Dancing, melts.

    Hopeless snowfall but.
    No joke.
    First of the season.

Where the mosquito-net dance sinks.
In an olive-dark inlet.
Seagulls riot.

On the far shore.
Opposite.

Fuji burns.

1970

On Peach Day Peach Blossoms
On Peach Day* I view peach blossoms.
And also the yellow of rape blossoms.

March 3.
No clouds in the heavens.

> White Fuji at noon blurred with peachblow.
> A beauty. Holding rape blossoms and peach blossoms to her breast.
> Came to visit my room

Old traditions live in the present.
How sweet it is.
On Peach Day I view peach blossoms.

Beside my sickbed.
In a white vase.
Peach blossoms.
Cast faint shadows on my face.

March 3 (Dolls' Festival Day) is also known as Peach Day

Winter Morning Walks
I like walks on winter mornings.
Because It's cold.
Because the chill stings & slices into my cheeks.
Because beside the road tea flowers are blooming.
Because Pen & Gen* are with me.
Because we don't meet anyone.
Because the trees are bare.
I know what it is to be bare. Because I feel I know this.
Cobalt grains on dragon cilia.
Because I can see at the northwest edge of the Chinese cabbage paddock Fuji
   immaculately white.
   Tobacco & bread. Not open yet?
   Hello hello. Bread & tobacco.
   Not open yet?
   (Gen Pen. Wait a bit more.)
   Excuse me. 5 boxes of 'Black Hi-Lite' & a loaf of bread. Sorry for getting you up so early. No. That's OK.
Turning at the thick-stemmed bamboo grove.
From all directions light explodes stabbing at me like spears.
A row of wheat amongst the frost. A row of green.
I like walks on winter mornings.
Because through the thin ice you can't see the mud in the ditch.
Because the sky is made of special glass &.
The moon is a thin slice of bruised radish.
Because the zelkova branches are strangely warm & smoky.
A red scattering of holly &.
Because the genuine plum blossoms are swelling.
Because the velvet of the cucumber blossoms is swelling.
Swelling is good.
I like walks on winter mornings.
Because though I've only got one eye my left eye suffices.
At the edge of a thicket of various trees dead eulalia grass.
A bulbul cries.
My heart is full.
My head is empty.

Marvellous.
The pure cotton gloves I bought for 60 yen in Izu-Shimoda are perfect.
When I wipe away the frost with my gloves.
In a place like this a clover patch.
Bee nettles.
Springs begins in the very dead of winter.
Now in the middle of time too enormous no pause at all.
The earth is rotating round & round.
Hard to believe.
My base solid.
I like walks on winter mornings.
Fields.
Paddocks.
Roads.
Paths.
Over there a grove of assorted bare trees.
Newly-born clouds.
Morning moon.
Gen.
Pen.
Opposite.
White Fuji.

*Kusano Shinpei's two dogs.

Fuji
Fuji does not think.
Thinking creatures think of Fuji but Fuji does not think.
Simply exists.
Big deep heavy.
&.
A soaring harmonic.

Clouds move.

As if symbolic of time itself.
Trapped in moving time Fuji.
Does not move however.
Rock-hard. Silent.

Then bathed by.
First sunlight.

From heaven the moon.
Pours down.

Volcano Fuji
New Year at Toro Village
Looking from Toro on the banks of the Abe river.
Fuji's smoke curls upwards into the pale-blue heavens.
(Happy New Year Happy New Year.)
The snow bathed in the morning sun glows alpine-rose.

Happy New Year Happy New Year.
How grassy is Wakamatsu's green.
How plump are the breasts of little girls.
Oh me oh my.

A giant pot.
Bursting fit to bust with hooch.
Serpentine beads all-a-sparkle.

Men and women alike hair everywhere.
Men and women alike drinking one after another from a huge *Sue* bowl.
Oh me oh my.

If they venture outside their huts at dusk.
Fuji's pillar of fire.
(Happy New Year Happy New Year.)
Ascending straight to the heavens.

1971

Dragon Fuji 1
Above Fuji.
A marquise reclines.
Her silk clothing touched with white.

Now from the horizon at the end of the vast far-off cloud.
The sun slips upward.

Half of Fuji is purple.
The cloud is dyed pink.

The sleeping dragon coils the marquise around itself.
Lifts its head.
Opens its mouth GHA.
Swallows the morning sunlight.

Dragon Fuji 2
Full moon.
In the heavens above Fuji.
Dragon space.

Eight dragons ruby eyes glittering.
Scales glistening blue & moist.
Bending curling looping.

Looping loop-the-loop.
SHOO SH'PPON
SHOO P'SSH

Looping loop-the-loop.

One dragon spits out a golden ball &.

The other seven one after another.
In the light of the full moon eight balls like arrows.
Fall into the celadon vastness.
Of earthly Fuji.

Cloud Sea Fuji
Columning cloud-fleece.
Wraps Fuji.
Columns created one after another.
Move silently northward.

As if soaking up to the neck in a spa steambath.
Fuji quietly closes its eyes.

Harmony.
Of movement and stillness.

Fuji's perpendicular rooted deeper and deeper.
Warmed through falls silent.

1973

Fuji
At the shoulder.
The cloud is torn.
Somehow quietly enraged.
In a blue sky.
At the base of the beautiful blue firmament.

1974

Dream Fuji
Belching fire.
The colour of winter-cherry.

> From the upward thrust of submarine strata? From geological stresses? From the logic of a not illogical natural physiology?

Belching fire.

> Accompanied by earthquakes.
> Lava forcing Fuji-basalt upwards.

Belching mauve fire.

> The sea too a sensuous pink.

Belching fire.

> The roar cannot be heard from here but.
> It burns black the dome of heaven.

1975

Chocho San
From the US military base at Makamenaya on 99 mile beach.
A plane with a cylindrical beacon attached to it takes off.
Into the blue skies over the sea.
Practice rounds explode 2 or 3 times make white dumplings.

At that time I.
Was searching for the remains of the house Takamura Chieko* once convalesced in.
On a village path.

Shaking the earth an armoured car mounted with an anti-aircraft gun has approached.
On its gun barrel in white paint is written 'Chocho san'.
The armoured car raised clouds of dust, I took off my ancient hat.
Covered my face with it.
'Chocho san'.
Could not possibly mean 'butterfly'.
Hammered onto the eaves of a shabby house newly-renovated was a sign 'Bar Makame'
but. Was this the name of a hostess there her brown cheeks covered with thick white
makeup or did it mean Madame Butterfly?

The base had been handed back.
Now there wasn't even barbed wire.

At the back of a crowd watching a bullfight in the Okinawa countryside a barrel bearing
the name 'Chocho san' unexpectedly appeared.
This was however a dream I dreamt last night.

Where is that anti-aircraft gun? Now?
In the gleaming steel double-barrelled muzzles.
Is Fuji's white belly reflected?

*Takamura Chieko (1886-1938): Western-style painter, wife of the celebrated poet
Takamura Kōtarō (1883-1956) who wrote a book of poetry about her, <u>Chieko Shō</u>
(1941)

Full moon Dragon
Twelve talons twelve toes four legs.
Twelve twisted ice-axes.
KI-KYOON KI-KYOON KI-KYOON
On the snow-wall of Fuji's slope.

Scales glittering blue torso.
Makes S, a straight line, again S, a straight line.
SHAH SHAH SHAH SHAH SHAH SHAH SHAH SHAH
Far far off.
Two cilia do as they please.
Romping & slapping snow.
Two-toned snowsmoke flares up.

In the heavens above white porcelain Fuji.
Lemon full moon.

Winter-cherry eyeballs suddenly open hard.
A fat tail lashes Fuji.
Whole body rose.
Vertically into the air.

In that instant.
Inside the tranquil dome of heaven.
The dragon becomes a rod.
A dagger.

A solitary black bean.
A black sesame seed.
Right into the heart of the full moon.
Going.
Gone.

Fuji Above the Clouds
From on board a plane
Below from about the 5th station all over.
Light heavy ash-grey.
Waves & waves of cloud.

The sun has already.
Set.

Massive.
Upside-down earthenware mortar.
Grey-black.

Sea Fuji
Beneath the surface.
Of the wine-dark sea.

Sinking heavily.
Metallic tower.

Wild cherry-blossom skin smooth.

Bathed in morning.
Brilliance.

All.
Of it.

Fuji
A snowslide on Fuji swallowed the lives of 15 students in a matter of seconds.
This mountain unlike any other in Japan.
Fuji does not believe that a column of monks are too heavy.
Nor that a mountain observatory is too noisy.
Sometimes clouds furry like mufflers wind round and round Fuji.
Sometimes classic pince-nez clouds float close by.
In the sea of trees even snow-grouse have multiplied.
The Ōsawa landslide must have carved out a huge mass of mountain.
That too does not bother Fuji.
Leaving everything to humanity and physics.
Before long it may yet poke out again a tongue of fire.
That too is left to nature.
Fuji is there.
Fuji simply exists.
Heaven overhead always.

Glass Moon
In the heavens.
Above bronze Fuji.

Crescent moon.
Made of glass.

Dream Fuji
As always Fuji.
Spouting fire the colour of Jack-o'-lantern.

No sign of it here but.
In the far far darkness of night.
A sudden blizzard hit the mountain top.

Raising smack in the centre a fiery pillar.
A rainbow arch of 5 colours.
Reaching to the heavens.

1976

Mt Fuji
From two factory smokestacks.
Smoke pillowing upwards.
A fake cloud travelling south.

Beyond the modern.

Hard.
Silver sublimity.

Fuji Instant
A red-madder.

Upside-down opening iron fan.

In the heavens.
Black indigo.

Fuji About to Sink into the Night
Within the sharp outline.
Of mortar.
Ash-purple.

Expanding sideways flat.
Spluttering vermilion.

31 December 1975 5:05-09 p.m.

Spreading out above still further.
Spluttering cerulean.

On the west porch of the 5th floor of the No. 3 ward of the Musashi Sakai Red
 Cross Hospital.
Wind blasting away.
Reeling I made a grab for the rail.
About the same height as myself.
Opposite ash-purple.
A silent weight a fixed fan.

Both sides of the corridor are festooned with bulbs &
                                                    | NO VISITORS |

Taking a deep breath I try.
To close the heavy steel door quietly but just pulling it does not work.

This year's last.
CRASH reverberated all around me.

1977

Mt Fuji
Black.
Upside-down earthenware mortar.

All around.
Sekine Shōji's.*
Vermilion.

*Sekine Shōji (1899-1919) Western-style painter known for his extraordinary colours.

Black Fuji
Sharply black.
At back of Fuji opposite.
Thousands of blue devils assemble.
From their bamboo blowpipes.
Simultaneously with all their might.
Streaming over Fuji from all directions.
Yellow red vermilion flames.
Explode.
Fire dragon.

A Distant View of Fuji
Opening my 2nd floor window all at once stunning yellow & green *Magnolia hypoleuca*. Japanese pagoda trees. Metasequoia. Laurel.
6 a.m. swimming in the innocent light.
Yellow & green leaves swaying in the breeze.

Until late last night.
Leaves drenched in torrential rain & wind from the typhoon.
This morning eloquent chatter of yellow & green.
Bathed in brilliant sunshine.

Visible from balcony clothes-line.
Far above an oak forest.
A full view first for a long time of ash-blue Fuji.
Above a pale pale cerulean.

Still closer to the cerulean.
Even with my one eye I can see a swarm of grey dragonflies.
(Last night where & what they were doing I don't know.)
Shooting upwards almost as if they had lost their senses.

1979

Dream Fuji
At that time.
Fuji was under the sea.
Neither was there sardine nor mackerel nor plankton.
At that time Fuji.
Spat up magma the colour of winter-cherry.
Magma & sea-blue mingled.
Simmering violet bubbles breaking.
Breaking directly above Fuji.
Phantasmagoria.
Steaming on the surface of the sea.
A thick volume of cloud swelling.
What possibly could it be.
Two mammoths side by side blankly wondering.
Staring.

Mulligan Stew Feast
12 Nov. 1977 from morning & all day — a cloudless sky.
Just right for a mulligan stew feast.
After 10 a.m. S turned up, then H, W & also (woman) S.
Today's lot have all been connected to the farm.
Mulligan stew's at night, before that, some heavy jobs.
1. Removing the red bricks on the west side of the garden & digging from there to the concrete fence transplant *zephyranthus candida* to the edges.
2. Beside the compost pit dig another hole & put the flowerpots into it.
3. Beside them arrange red bricks in a row & make a common grave for the animals.
4. Pull up the eggplants. In their place sow silver beet & garden-pea seeds.
5. Dig up the taro.
6. Shift the earth dug out of the holes to the rose garden.
7. On the east side make an oven with bricks and rocks.
8. Take the dead leaves from the garden to the compost pot.
9. Clean out the pond, do the weeding etc.

Everyone grabbed spades, hoes & pruning shears & began to work.
The old man from Koenuma brought bundles of straw on his bicycle to protect the peonies against frost.
We were covered in sweat, bathed in the sunlight from a cloudless sky.
Time for a breather.
Spreading 2 mats on the paddock we sit cross-legged.
Slurping hot noodles.
Then back to work.
We go & get a long plank from a nearby builder & cut it with a saw.
Give it a good scrub & dry it in the sun.
Upstairs I write on a grave-marker.

Kōzō Fū Kū Gen Pen Tonko

KUSANO FAMILY TOMB

Black Fuji & the rest all the fishes Amen

Into a gap in the square of red brick. I hammer it deeply.
The work in the paddock and garden is mostly finished.
I set fire to some dead wood in our improvised oven.
W brought thick pieces of charcoal from the cellar.
A rare treat in times like our own.
Chucked them over 4 or 5 pieces of burning wood.
On top of that plonked a massive iron pot 62 cms in diameter & filled with water.
Tables & giant *saké* bottles & beer & glasses & chopsticks.
We all split up to carry them.
The water in the iron pot had boiled & was chattering & bubbling away.
The seasoning was my responsibility.
First Shinshū miso paste & chopped pork.
Then in the pot went most respectfully the taro radish & mustard rape dug up this morning.
Next in no particular order came the food in baskets & on trays.

Burdock. carrots. Tōfu. Chinese Cabbage. Cabbage. Mushrooms. Devil's tongue.
Kidney Beans. Challots. Komatsuna Cabbage.
I tasted some from a small dish. On top I poured beer & *saké*.
& a few tiny drops of soy sauce.
First I put some half-boiled vegetables & rice into a bowl & placed it on the
    Kusano family tomb as an offering.
Just then simply & directly we.
Toasted each other with beer & *saké*.
A big steaming bowl was passed from hand to hand.
After that came eating & drinking. Drinking & eating.
The sun was already orange & was about to sink on the southern flank of Fuji.
The giant size candles bought at Tsubekawa in Izu were brought out.
Also a big square candle pink & white & light blue all mixed together made for
    me by a young woman I didn't know.
Anyhow we all unabashedly.
Scream out 'tastes great' 'lovely'.
So it ought.
After the work an open-air feast.
But we couldn't eat everything in the massive 62 cm pot.
Ended up getting the neighbours in to share it.
Sun set & candlelight flared.
Bodies & faces glowed.
Moon came up.
Charcoal crackled.
Carefully dowsed the fire.
Afterwards decided to continue the party upstairs.

Mt Fuji
From the becalmed horizon.
When an innocent round fire-mass.
Sprang smoothly upwards.
Sunlight slid over an expanse of cloud.
Sliding outwards.
From above the sixth station.
Pale silent Fuji.
In an instant.
Flashed.
Coral-pink.
The powder-blue heavens opened wide.

Fountainhead Fuji
Once Fuji's entrails.
Were a fiery powder magazine.
Now openings are scattered about randomly.
From its roof drops of water drip.
Underground water flows between the mud bed of ancient Fuji and the lava bed of
    modern Fuji.
    (The powder magazine has metamorphised into an underground fountainhead.)
Flowing guttering zigzag from a cliff near the mountain's foot.
Fountains glitters palely to fall downwards.
Falls downwards all night all day.
    (white thread waterfall: less than useless as a name.)
And sometimes.
Spits rainbows.

Mare's Tail Fuji
Was it monkey *saké* that the 8-headed dragon of Yawata drank?
Or was it red honeysuckle *saké* made by humans?
Such were the absurd notions I was entertaining while.
Drinking cold *saké*.
In the latter half of the 20th century.
Thinking about the age of the *Kojiki* * from a distance.
(The more *saké* you drink the more you want — so they say.)
A *kimono* is tanned Japanese bearhide.
A padded sleeveless *kimono* jacket is wild blue boar hide.
Posing anyway I want.

(The more *saké* you drink the more you want — so they say.)
Venturing out onto my 1st floor veranda.
Ah fantastic.
Vermilion mare's tail cloud.
Directly below Fuji worse luck cannot be seen but.
Lifting my glass through the mare's tail cloud.
In one swallow I drink to all of my 75 years.

**The oldest historical chronicle of Japan presented to the Empress Gemmei in 712 A.D.*

1980

Magnificent Dragon
Floating in the light of the full moon cilia & scales glitter green.
Skimming over the sea a magnificent dragon.
Heads south deliberately.

Suddenly.
Fierce thunder explodes in the north.
Glancing back.
A fat crimson pillar of fire from Fuji a moment ago touched the sky.
In an instant the dragon gulping a belly full of seawater.
At full tilt.
Whipping cilia strike at the dark air.
Face Fuji & thrust inwards.

(The magnificent dragon & Fuji are no ordinary companions.)

On its water-soaked face & body.
Carmine-red glistening.
Abruptly leapt to the heavens above Fuji.

Aiming at the dragon.
Molten volcanic rock hurtles upward.
The magnificent dragon spearing straight at the fiery pillar spat water but.
The dragon was blanketed by thick steam.

In a cave on a southern island.
Singed cilia dipped in blue water.
The dragon muttered to itself.
'Though we may be no ordinary companions. I am me. Fuji is Fuji. Let mountains look after mountain matters. Spit more & more magnificent fire!'

1981

Undersea Fantasy
Sea snow like feathered insects.
In the dark cavern of the sea without pause.
Falling falling falling falling.

Catching the sea snow.
Heaping it up.
Stretching vast, long & impressive.
The chain of the Himalayas.

At the end of the distant Pacific.
Fuji spills red viscous magma everywhere.
Within swirls of thick violet smoke.
Grows big & fat.

Fuji Fantasy
5 a.m.

Ancestor of the field horsetail.
Clematis concealed in a great forest.

Rose.
Fuji.

Pale.
Rose.
Pince-nez cloud.

Fuji at 77

1

From Lake Sagami.
Perfectly cloudless.
And transparent cerulean.
At centre crystal-clear.
Fuji two-thirds snow.
Have I ever seen such a beautiful, peaceful Fuji?
Unexpectedly I am.
The owner of only one eye.
I thought over the joys of one living eye.
But to no avail.
Fluid filled my living eye.
Fuji was caught in the blur.

2

We climbed slowly halfway up.
Two women.
Eight men in an open-air banquet.
Plonking round hard snow into wineglasses.
Riceballs and a cornucopia of side-dishes.
Toasting each other in frozen clinks.
Yet imagine this.
In the vast heavens cloudless a moment ago.
Cirrus clouds are created, unusual for May.
Near the edge of their creation pince-nez clouds.
Superimposed on an eye resting from sketching.
Silk thread oblique straight white jet-wake line of cloud.
About the banquet.
A birch and a rhododendron bush scattered over the hard sheet of snow.

3
In the restaurant *Tsukasa* by the shore of Lake Kawaguchi.
I had raw cucumber, tomato, *tempura* with dried cod and raw horse meat.
As a side-dish.
Beer beer beer.
On 12 May 1980 77 years of age I alone.
Scoffed a three-quarters-full glass of tortoise blood.

4
Ten of us.
A former Seibu traindriver.
A guy who fronted as the proprietor of a Mah-Jong parlour.
A clerk at a publishing firm.
A minor employee of a foreign trading company.
The guard at a certain bank.
A workaholic 'tinkling in the breeze'.
A hodgepodge of assorted odds and ends.

5
At the last riverside fishmarket in Akitsu.
Beer. Johnny Walker Black. Japanese *saké*.
A Tosa chef's raw bonito seared and sliced.
We started by imitating a Kabuki actor's delivery.
And ended with everyone taking turns to sing.

Eating Snow

From Teshirozawa back of Nikkō two horse-chestnut trees and.
From Tadeshina *akebi* and metasequoia.
From Abukuma *magnolia hypoleuca* and Japanese pagoda-trees and winged spindle-
    trees and.
From Chichibu purple azaleas.
Musashino zelkovas snowbells oaks maples.
All with bare bark and branches.
This year. First snow in the neighbourhood.
Soft soft soft soft snowing thick.
A bulbul cries.

(Then we drank the snow's health with *saké*)

Feast your eyes on this morning's snow on garden and paddock.
Bathed in brilliant sunshine.
Here & there diamond-particles glisten.
Gently falling onto straw baskets protecting peonies and chinquapin logs growing
    mushrooms.
Carp swim quietly in a scattering of blue reflections.
If I stand on the verandah the middle of the table's piled up high.
With masses of snow fallen on the lump of lava brought from the shores of Lake Sai.
Base over apex the white mortar of.
Crisp Fuji there also.
In my right hand I grab snow hard outside soft inside.
Shove it in my mouth.
Heaven-sent transparent clean non-taste.

The Japanese Archipelago
The skyline of the Japanese archipelago.
Is the horizon of the Pacific Ocean.

> Continuing the cry of innocence across a quarter of a century. A sixty-eight year old housewife finally dying of disease. The false testimony of two young clerks extracted by torture by the prosecution.
> Parents murdering children. Children murdering parents. Grabbing a gun in a bank. Vile vile vile vile. Violent gangs.
>
> Business-expense paradise highest in history (entertainment allowance expenditure totalling 2.9 trillion yen. Political donations 2 billion yen.) Etc. Etc.
>
> The title politician ceased to exist in the Meiji era.
> Society is complex and grotesque. Crimes of the cross proliferate in broad daylight. Every year murky affairs of every variety increase.

1981 morning sun at least.
Slide up from the horizon.
& dye white porcelain Fuji the colour of multi-petaled cherry blossoms.

1982

Blue Fuji
Beneath the full moon.
A thumping deep heavy hard.
Broad-bottomed.
Bronze-like Fuji.
Furry clouds wrapped round its base.
White blue ghostly.

The skies above the neighbourhood of distant Tokyo.
With a faint brightness are at peace but.
Demons with human faces prowl silently.
Suddenly blood spurts.
Demons with human faces dart zigzag.

As if sadness & anger were thrown together.
The abrupt sound of an explosion.
Blue Fuji.
A single glass-grained rod thick & strong.
Aimed right at the centre of the firmament.
Jets upwards.

Seabed Fuji
The ceiling here is the horizon. It should be prussian blue rolling rolling placidly but. Smoking all the while magma jelly dribbles down the steep slope of the mountain. To the horizon-ceiling dark tan peacock-coloured red-madder transparent winter-cherry great gurgling asthma. Hot hot waves rolling rolling smoke pluming upwards. Under the sea utter chaos. Magma jelly rising upwards to the horizon. Steaming into mushrooming mushrooming smoke. Rainbow coloured. As if to say 'I'm a god' twisting twisting climbing climbing climbing.

Fuji Hallucination

   dddd   dddddddd   duggaan
   uuuu   nn   uwaan

Bright red.
Sporting a fine big moustache the sun.

From the left belly of Fuji.
Above the pillar of new-spouting magma.
Rolls & rolls.

   ddd   dddd   uuuu   gaggaan

Surely not now in the 20th century.
Would Fuji explode all its pent-up rage in one stroke.

An utterly different proposition from that kind of common sense or the lack of it. Yet.
An explosion is an explosion.

Purple firmament waves all-a-riot.

   bun   bun   bun   bun
   un   uwn   nnnnnnn   nnn

Red Cross Fuji

6 o'clock exactly. A nurse hands me a thermometer. And says 'Mt Fuji is very pretty this morning.'

I walk along the slippery corridor from the east to the west wing on the 5th floor of ward 3 and open the door. Rest against the steel railing.

1 minute 2 minutes 3 minutes.

(Fuji just the same.)

4 minutes. 5 minutes.

I saw it on 12 May last year.
I wonder.
If I'll be able to see the same Fuji again.

Hmm?
That's the Chichibu mountain range.

5 minutes. 6 minutes. 7 minutes 8 minutes.

Hard existence rough white stripes against purple.
Yet.
Without the drama of the heavens in the background Fuji would not exist.

So I affirm once again.

9 minutes.

Will I go back? I'm sore.
It's not my right hand.

Ah forgive me.

1983

Giant China Carp
I
Early in the morning 12 May 1982.
Noisy voices in my garden.
I came down from the first floor and a giant China carp looking over 100 centimetres in size was about to be released from a plastic bag into my carp pond.
I don't know about the Yangtze River.
Even in Lake Hsuan-wu I've never seen one as mighty as this.
The noisy voices were the old man who runs an art supply shop. A bank clerk. Driver. Mah-jong proprietor. Three young editors in a publishing firm. An employee of a foreign trading company.
(A birthday present.)
Someone said.
Straightaway I named him '79'.
(On this day next year I'll rename him '80'.)
Everyone laughed.

Now it's getting ready to leave time. Two women. Nine men. In two cars to the 5th station of Fuji. My annual birthday celebration. Making a circle in a clearing on the hard snow. A small but splendid banquet.

II
Abebe who died eight years ago was a long lanky black carp.
He reminded me of the African marathon runner so I named him 'Abebe'.
Abebe was always in some way or another on his own.

> Buying a big bunch of pussy-willow at the end of the year has been a family tradition for many years. It then becomes the sole decoration in our *toko no ma* *. January February March comes. White velvet releases yellow pollen. Light-green buds begin to sprout. Before you're hardly aware of it pure white roots thinner than vermicelli have sprouted and are sucking up the water in the vase.

I dug a hole with a shovel in a corner of my paddock.
Buried Abebe.

Placing one sprig of pussy-willow on the corpse.
Sprinkling eau de Cologne over him.
Every year the pussy-willow grew but.
I suddenly took it into my head to.
Transplant it between the *magnolia hypoleuca* and metasequoia in my garden.
Sadly the pussy-willow died.
It should have been with Abebe.

III

79 is a carp but in personality he resembles Abebe in many respects.
Thrown in among sixteen carp of all colours.
As well as 79 I've got *Mahakala* and Big Black both big and totally black in colour.
If I scatter synthetic fishfood about the carp toss up spray and polish it off in no time all but.
79 remains aloof.

That's only natural.
Essentially 79's food is water plants. From rivers and lakes.
I suddenly slapped my knee.
I cull some sprouts of buckchoy from the row in my paddock as both* come from the same single homeland. Tear off the roots and toss them in the pond. The carp eat them but 79 just approached and did not even attempt to have a nibble.

Yesterday afternoon for whatever reason.
He finally ate some.
This morning too. And he really seemed to enjoy it.
23rd day since he was released into the pond.
While pleased as punch.
That he'd eat in my tiny pond not a lake.
Not water plants but a product of his homeland buckchoy from my house.
For me my second homeland. Its vastness overwhelmed me.

* *toko-no-ma* : *A recess or alcove in a Japanese style room where valuable hanging scrolls or heirlooms are kept.*
*both: carp and buckchoy

1984

Fuji's Garments
Nothing artificial.
Fuji is an entity of the physical universe.
The garments enfolding it are all all.
Natural scientific products.

   Cloud·Light·Darkness·Moon·Space·Sunlight.

Once mammoths disported themselves in sexual frolics watching.
Fuji's fire pillar.
Now. In the ultramarine of the 1980s.

   Stratus·Strato-cumulus·Cannonball cloud·Fishing-line cirrus· Pince-nez cloud.

The fairy-tale hare in the full moon is a craggy mountain range.

The blue desert beside.
Time flows.

   Crescent moon·Glass moon.
   & full full. Another full moon.

The blood-covered ball of morning from Pacific Ocean horizon.
Slides into view.
The snow on Fuji's peak.
Faint rose-colour.
Before the sun sets in the west endless series of changes.

   Horizontal straight line of gold cloud.
   Crazy red.
   Mushrooms mushrooms.

& Fuji.
Clothed in the pale airy garments of a marquise.

But in the tranquillity of deep sleep.
Transparent water-vein within does not sleep.
Spouts into five lakes.
From its centre a small waterfall springs outwards.
This great nature even while sleeping does not sleep.

Mt Fuji
Straight down deep inside.

>   Storing up fire & water &.
>   A mass of rage.

Fuji is.
Silent.

Fuji on a morning in March
The whole is a harsh white but.
Transparent blue &.
Pale crimson combine.
Fuji's cone.

>   A momentary phase from an infinite variety.

In the light-blue space over Japan.
Not even a 13 year-old virgin.
Cloud.

Extraordinary
A whale in the South Seas.
Turns into a dragon.

Aiming at Fuji.

Distant.
Celadon.

China Carp and My Birthday
If I open the window on the 3rd floor of the new wing.
Of Musashi Sakai Red Cross Hospital & poke my head out.
In the distant north white porcelain Fuji appears clearly.
For the past 3 days today too.
Silvery snow-white in the far off cerulean sky.

(It's already the 14th day since evening drinking has changed to eating in my diary.)

12 May is my birthday.
On the hard snow halfway up Fuji if we have a banquet this year it'll be number 5.
All around 20 or 30, a younger lot than me. Usually 5 men 2 women.
That day is drawing closer.

Looking at distant Fuji.
There's no direct connection but '79' the China carp in my small pond.
How's he doing? I remembered.

On my birthday last year. The young lot released into my pond a giant China carp they had loaded onto a truck.
At that time straightaway I named him 79 after my age. When I remarked next year at this time I'll rename him 80 everybody burst into happy laughter.

12 May is drawing closer. (Last year at about this time I was in a room of a 27th floor apartment in Honolulu painting pastels almost every day but this year stuck in hospital.)

Nevertheless today is the 14th of March. I should be leaving hospital on the 20th so everything's OK.
I wonder will I go on a trip to Fuji again?
This year I might change my plans a little.
Go & see the elephants giraffes lions & all the rest.

Along the way.
Pawlonia's purple. Magnolia's white & globeflower's yellow.
Rhododendron's vermilion & wistaria's purple.
& at the foot of the mountain Fuji-cherry blossoms' pale crimson.

Incidentally 79 at home.
On 12 May you too will turn 80 with me.
Even if it's not your favourite water-hyacinths.
At least I'd like to find some hornwort by the Yanase river.
To celebrate the first day of your 80th year.

Once again gazing steadily at pure white Fuji.
I'm going to get dressed.
Change into Western clothing complete with bow-tie & wait for the nurse.
Then set out for the meeting where the school song of the Musashi College of Nursing
    is to be announced.
Lyrics: Shinpei · Music: Akutagawa Yasushi.
By the way the school song of the Red Cross Junior College (as it's known) on the same campus also has lyrics by Shinpei · Music by Dan Ikuma.
A knock at the door & a nurse smiling sweetly comes into my room.
I get into the wheelchair the nurse is pushing.
Descend by elevator to the ground floor.
I am surrounded by Himalayan cedars.
In the direction of the college building 'in the round'.
Right underneath the 'indigo heavens' 'limitless light'.
Transported in a ludicrously absurd way.
Slightly embarrassed but.
Nothing I can do about it.

At the Musashi Sakai Red Cross Hospital

1985

Fuji Dreamscape
Suddenly.
A huge.
Sound.

Far far off.
On the pale dark horizon.
Crimson-purple.
Fat fire-pillar.

A single line.
Slipping over the sea's surface.

Reflecting the fire-pillar.
In the heavens.
A red full moon.

Mt Fuji
No matter which of the mountains in the world.
Mountains change.
That is the destiny of mountains.

    Because of the Ōsawa landslide Fuji grew thin.
    Because of eruptions Fuji grew grossly fat.
    That happened 277 years ago in the Hōei era.
    Both were Fuji's destiny.

    It is not a subject for debate by representatives.
    In that tiny stone hut called the 'Diet'.
    Ferroconcrete.
    With that Fuji is Fuji (irreparable).

But as the symbol of Japan Fuji is Fuji (unique).
Its infinite beauty.
Varies according to changes in the celestial sphere.

Record of My Baths 1983-4
Two o'clock in the morning New Years Day 1983.
Entering the cypress bath at home.
Giving myself a good scrub with a brush.
After that a full month with no bath.
No bath in February.
No bath in March.
No bath in April.
No bath in May.
Once in June. This time also a good scrub with a brush.
Then again no bath in July.
No bath in August.
In September I had 3 baths at Tenzan Library*
This time too no loofah. Good scrub with a brush.
At the end of the month I returned to Tokyo but.
No bath in October.
No bath in November.
No bath in December.
I thought I'd refresh myself on New Years Eve but. Still no bath.
I slid into 1984.
Once more no bath in January.
No bath in February.
No bath in March.
No bath in April.
11 May. The next day was my 81st birthday.
As usual I reckoned on climbing to the 5th station of Mt Fuji but (somehow my body felt limp, funny. I was urged on by everybody. Prompted by remarks like 'we'll go with you'. I went to the Red Cross Hospital at Musashi Sakai). Right in the middle of the check-up. Dreaming of 'Bottoms up!' with the young crew of the Fuji Society on mats on the hard snow at the 5th station of Mt Fuji I insisted on not being admitted to hospital but. Though we had known each other for some time the doctor-in-charge would not permit it. I ended up lying in bed on the 3rd floor. Diary entry for 24 May ⑥
Big happening (bath=scrubbing brush)
I had a bath as I was in my private room.
Adding it up it was my first bath in 246 days.
My whole body. I felt as if my skin had grown thin.

Clouds drifted past the window beside the bed in which I lay.

*

Occasionally even for me there were exceptions.
For example when I stayed in the Bandai Atami inn.
I had a bath 3 times in one day & afternoon & evening.
A 45 kilo bag of bones but.
Just enough hot water rushing over me.
Sounding good & clean.
Marvellous.

    Some friends advised me.
    How about renovating the bathroom?
    Sinking the cypress bathtub down into the floor.
        Didn't you renovate the balcony where you dried clothes to make a studio with a
            glass roof?
    (You should sink the high cypress bathtub lower into the floor.)
    So I should.
    But I have one more small dream.
    Beside the glass roof of the studio.
    On the ground-floor roof tiles.
    I want to build a glass observatory to view Fuji.
    A tiny square one that only one person can enter.
        To build one you need what you need.
        To build two you need twice as much.
        To build both at this point in time I need to think about further.

*

24 May I had a bath at the Musashi Sakai Red Cross Hospital.
Today is 16 July.
(52nd day with no bath.)
But today the Tenzan festival is over.
When all of a sudden my accumulated fatigue disappears.
My unconscious awareness of not having had a bath will be blown away.

I'll try to have a bath at the Library.
Immersing myself up to my head in lukewarm water.
In the bathroom a good scrub with a brush as usual.
I'll sluice myself with reams of hot water.

*

In toto I was in hospital for 40 days but.
Today I'll finally be released.
12 August.
The day I'm to be released from the Joint Iwaki General Hospital.
Yesterday I gave myself a very very gentle scrub with a brush. First bath in 80 days.

   For the first time in ages.
   Tonight at the Library.

At long last I drink a small glass of cold *saké*.
Rationing myself to just two drinks.
Next morning.
Basking in the light from the Abukuma mountains.
I rush to the umpteenth *obon* * baseball meet at Kawauchi village.
The opening ceremony for the 19 village teams and the tradition of my pitching the first
    ball.
Day after tomorrow at the coming-of-age ceremony a super-short speech.
And after that.
And after that.
The dog's breakfast of my piled-up work.

*

I feed 33 carp.
Strolling about my garden pruning shears and saw in hand.
6 October.
Completely forgot about having a bath.
Counting on my fingers.
Its been 55 days.

55 days since I've had a bath but.
I haven't felt the slightest urge to do so.

    The leaves of the azalea have turned vermilion.
    The osmund fern has turned yellow.
    The leaves of the *magnolia hypoleuca* have become pock-marked.

Oy. Dragon-fly flying over there.
Dragon-fly.
Where're you going?
The sky at the onset of autumn.
Is incredibly high!
I'm tired. Ah tired.
I'll go back to my 6 mat room with the heater.

I fell flat-out onto the bed.

    If I call my singlet a shirt.
    I've got on 3 shirts.

        On top of that a navy-blue woollen shirt.
        Two jumpers.
        A padded sleeveless vest
        That's what I was wearing.

Quietly on my own I made up my mind.
In good health.
Naturally.
And full of life.
Until I have a mind to.
Not to have a bath.

*Tenzan Library: the Kusano library in the mountains west of Tokyo to where the poet frequently retreated.
*obon : mid-summer festival celebrating the return home of the ancestral spirits.

Mt Fuji
From Fuji's belly.
Pure water flows.
There may be times when it boils.
A lava stream perhaps.

The gods do not know this.
It is Fuji's destiny.
Nor does Fuji know.

1986

Red Cross Fuji
From the 3rd floor verandah here.
I can clearly see Fuji as high as the hairline on my forehead.
That velvety white.
The same pedigree as the indigo of the vegetable-dyed pongee gown I'm now wearing.
So many times·so many times·so many times·so many times·so many times.
Have I seen Fuji.
So many times·so many times·so many times.
Have I seen Fuji.
the head nurse I knew 24 years ago. Now in the lobby she seems to be the boss of the whole hospital.
  That's how it was.
  Umezaki Haruo*. Tsuji Makoto.
  It was me who introduced them to this hospital.
  That drunkard.
  That mountain climber.
  Are no more.
  Haniya Yutaka's* wife has died too.
  While I was in hospital.
  For me but.
      Both *Namu Amida Butsu* *
      & Amen were not for me.
      Not now either.

*

Above damson-plum coloured Fuji.
Dark pince-nez clouds are floating.
The eroticism of a small twist.
In the belly.
An invitation of how many years I wonder?
Since I saw it on the slopes of Akagi.
Ah.

*

Fuji is fixed.
Without expression.

However around the pubic bone & pelvis.
Sputtering lava flow vortex.
Water flows over its belly bursts BAH from its side.
Stomach is void.
Yet. Nevertheless.
If the body shakes.
Smoke strong & hot.
Lotus-red flame.
    GONWANGONWANGOGONWANWAN
    GONWANGONWANGOGONWANWAN
    Twisting dancing lifting lotus-red flame.
    The entire firmament.
    Crazy red paddock.
    Of lotus-red flame.

*

Ah. I would have.
All at once clouds rush across the heavens.
Like ginsen a thousand lightnings hanging.
Flash & thunder! &.
Buckets & buckets & buckets & buckets of squalling rain.
Pelting pouring down buckets & buckets.
Buckets & buckets pelting pouring down.

*

Fuji is fixed.
February dawn Fuji.
Frozen & slippery.
Pale pink.•

<At zenith a pointed moon.>

Ah.
Frozen & slippery.
Upside-down mortar.
Pale pink.

* *Namu Amida Butsu : A standard Buddhist prayer.*
* *Umezaki Haruo (1915-1965) Novelist.*
* *Haniya Yutaka (1910-) Novelist.*

Something Something Fuji
Tsugaru Fuji.
Iwate Fuji.
O O Fuji.
X X Fuji.
□ □ Fuji.
Japan's countless.
Rich Samurai/Fuji*.
Countless Fujis.

Before the Jōmon era*.
No even earlier.
Before the birth of the human race.
In the very centre of the Japanese archipelago Japan's highest mountain.
   No two Fujis.
   Unique mountain. (Fuji)

They say it looks like that mountain.
Δ Δ Fuji.
O O Fuji.
Like a symbol of the yearning to be the centre, the power.
What.
Does something something Fuji mean?
That they resemble Fujis found here & there throughout Japan.
They do not resemble the Fuji.
I want to celebrate their beauty & power.
& in a quieter tone.
Without exception.
The independence of each & every one.

*'Rich Samurai' is a wordplay, a literal reading of the Chinese characters meaning Fuji. This in the text I gloss '/Fuji'.
*The Jōmon era is part of the old stone-age period in prehistoric Japan.

My Walk
Strolling.
Swaying swaying.
The path I'm strolling along now.
Originally was a desolate wintry paddy-field I think.
Around here where I'm flying a kite.
Gen & Pen used to play. Fishmonger's Kennedy too.
Kai-bred Gen.
Whippet-bred Pen both no longer among the living.
At the edge of my Gokō paddock.
Sleeping in the <Kusano Family Tomb>.
In those days after lighting a fire in the ditch between the paddy-fields.
I'd fly a kite a picture- postcard in the sky.
So now.
Legs wobbly.
One-eyed.
Hard of hearing.
If a car comes from behind.
I can't even hear the tyre sounds.
Everybody believes I can no longer go for walks by myself.
Before from shopping at the fishmonger general store greengrocer.
To cooking I was the boss but.
Now far from that.
One-eyed.
Hard of hearing.
Shoes too cloth-made.
Peking scuffs.
<Watch out for cars!>
Shopping strolling walking on my own is not permitted.
The path through the oak grove.
The path through the line of tea trees.
I could be accidentally knocked down by a child's bike.
Everything has strangely changed.
The occasional walk has come to an end &.
Climbing the stairs to the first floor with Leo* coming to greet me.
Without support is impossible.

Panting grasping the banister.
Even sitting cross-legged in my renovated studio on the balcony where the clothes used to dry.
I can't see Fuji.
Because of the buildings.

* Leo is the name of Kusano Shinpei's cat.

Translator's Afterword

Kusano Shinpei (1903-1988) was one of Japan's most distinguished twentieth-century poets. He was also one of the most productive, especially during the last fifteen or so years of his life when he tried to publish a new collection every year. That such a prolific poet should return to a number of recurring themes during a career spanning over six decades comes as no surprise. One of the most enduring of his themes was Mt Fuji.

Fuji has been celebrated in verse as a holy mountain, a mountain symbolic of Japan itself, since at least the eighth century when it appears as a theme in poetry collected in the *Manyōshū*, Japan's oldest collection of verse. It has also been celebrated in the plastic arts, most notably by the master of the wood-block print Katsushika Hokusai (1760-1849). Hokusai made two series of prints featuring Mt Fuji between 1831 and 1834 which achieved unparalleled heights of popularity. Kusano Shinpei's Fuji poems sometimes borrow images or motifs from Hokusai and sometimes borrow from the older tradition as well. But, for the most part, the poet's vision of Fuji is his own.

His first Fuji collection was published in 1943 and mostly consists of poems written during the previous three years. These years Kusano spent in Canton as an adviser to the puppet government of Wang Ching-wei (1883-1944). So the first incarnation of Fuji in the poet's work is, as might be expected from the tenor of the times, nationalistic. His nationalistic tone which reaches back into antiquity in its origins is tempered by elements of Pan-Asianism.[1] Kusano often referred to China as his 'second homeland', and his love for China and hopes for a Sino-Japanese comity are evident in this collection.

The only other single collection he published on Fuji, quite different in tone from the first, was in 1966 and consists of 18 poems written between 1951 and 1966. This collection was published with an English translation appended which is why it is not included in this volume. The translators of that second Fuji collection, Cid Corman and Kamaike Susumu, set an exceedingly high standard with their much-acclaimed renderings. I can only hope my versions have maintained the level

---

[1] For a detailed discussion of this and the second Fuji collection (1966) see my 'A Dragon Rising: Kusano Shinpei's Poetic Vision of Mt Fuji', *Journal of the Oriental Society of Australia* Vol. 17 (1985) pp.39-63.

of excellence they have established.[2] Since that collection, apart from a selection of Fuji poems (culled from earlier volumes) published in 1977, Kusano wrote no further collections specifically on the theme of Mt Fuji.[3]

But, as can be seen here, the majority of his Fuji poems were written after 1966. He continued his interest, perhaps one might argue obsession, with Fuji right up to the last collection he published before his death.

The later Fuji poems were all published in those volumes he managed to turn out almost every year during the last two decades of his life. As such their treatment of Fuji differs markedly from the earlier two Fuji collections. They reflect his growing concern with the issue of his own mortality, the joys and sorrows that age brings, and the sheer delight in life experienced by one who is in a position to appreciate its fleeting nature. These poems, I believe, are among the most profound and moving that he ever wrote. In his later years Kusano Shinpei achieved a freedom of expression and diction that lesser poets can only dream of. In some poems Fuji may seem incidental to a larger theme yet on closer inspection we can see that it acts as the pivot upon which the larger concern turns.

Kusano Shinpei may well be unique among his peers in pursuing one theme so intently throughout the course of his career. The intensity of his vision of Mt Fuji has compelled and delighted me for over six years now. I hope it may do the same for readers unable to savour the brilliance of the originals.

*

In making these translations I have been guided by two dictums: that the English be as faithful to the original Japanese as possible (translations not paraphrases) and that the translations work as poems in English. To fulfil the second aim I have departed on some occasions from the principle of consistency and have translated the same Japanese expression in a number of different ways. However as English in linguistic terms has practically nothing in common with Japanese this was inevitable. In his poetry Kusano often makes use of various onomatopoetic devices to startling effect and the Fuji poems are no exception. I have tried a variety of means to convey his literary pyrotechnics (often guided by the stunning successes

---

[2] Their translation was first published in *Fuji San* (Mt Fuji), Tokyo: Iwasaki Bijutsusha, 1966. But it is now available in vol.2 of the Collected Works (*Kusano Shinpei Zenshū*); for details consult the Bibliographic Note.

[3] That collection is *Fuji no Zentai* , Tokyo: Satsuki Shobō, 1977.

achieved by Corman and Kamaike) but much has been lost in translation. The poems translated here constitute all, to my knowledge, that he has written on the theme of Mt Fuji (interpreted in as liberal a way as possible) with the exception of the collection noted above, two other poems translated by Corman and Kamaike and another poem written in English by Kusano and published in 1979.[4] So virtually all the Fuji poems are translated into English here for the first time.

*

I wish to thank the following individuals for all their assistance and support: Hugh Clarke, Cid Corman, Fujita Makoto, Kris Hemensley, Kamaike Susumu, Robert Kenny, the late Kusano Shinpei, Matsui Sakuko, the late Mizutani Akio and last but not least my wife Sachiko.

Some of these translations have previously appeared in the following publications: *Journal of the Oriental Society of Australia* and *Tales From East of the River*.

---

[4] The other two poems on Fuji translated by Corman and Kamaike are 'Nihon Sabaku' (The Desert of Japan) and 'Tokyo Kōen' (Tokyo Park) both originally published in 1948. They are included in *frogs & others*, New York: Grossman Publishers [Mushinsha Press], 1969. There is also a third volume of Corman/Kamaike translations *asking myself/answering myself*, New York: New Directions Press, 1984.

Bibliographic Note

The *Kusano Shinpei Zenshū* [Collected Works], edited by Sō Sakon, Nakagiri Masao and Yamamoto Tarō (Tokyo: Chikuma Shobō, 1978-1984, 12 vols.) hereafter *KSZ*, makes up the basic reference set for poems taken from collections published up to 1980. Beginning with *Unki* [Cloud Passage], references after that date are made directly to the volumes in which the poems appear, as these volumes are not included in *KSZ*.

1. 1943: *Fuji San* [Mt Fuji]
   (Tokyo: Shōshinsha, 1944)
   Fuji San I-XVII   *KSZ* Vol.1 pp.281-304

2. 1944: *Daihakudō* [The Great White Road]
   (Tokyo: Kōtorishorin, 1944)
   Fuji San [Mt Fuji]   *KSZ* Vol.1 p.308
   Kuro Fuji [Black Fuji]   *KSZ* Vol.1 p.309

3. 1948: *Nihon Sabaku* [The Desert of Japan]
   (Tokyo: Seijisha, 1948)
   Fuji Kakkazan [Volcano Fuji]   *KSZ* Vol.1 pp.358-9
   Botan'en [Peony Garden]
   (Tokyo: Kamakura Shobō, 1948)
   Uchūsen Fuji [Cosmic Ray Fuji]   *KSZ* Vol.1 p.444

4. 1951: *Ten* [The Firmament]
   (Tokyo: Shinchōsha, 1951)
   Ten [Firmament]   *KSZ* Vol.2 p.104
   Fuji San 1-4 [Mt Fuji]   *KSZ* Vol.2 pp.143-7
   Fuji San ōi ni Azawarau [Mt Fuji Has a Big Laugh]   *KSZ* Vol.2 p.148

> Note; not included is:
> 1966:   *Fuji San* [Mt Fuji](Tokyo: Iwasaki Bijutsusha, 1966)   *KSZ* Vol.2 pp.285-331
> (See Translator's Afterword)

5. 1968: *Kowareta Orugan* [The Broken Organ]
   (Tokyo: Shōrinsha, 1968)
   Fuji Yo Warero! [Break Fuji Break!]   *KSZ* Vol.3 p.53 ff.
   Kyō mo Mata Hajimete no Fuji   *KSZ* Vol.3 p.57
      [Today too Fuji for the First Time]
   Tōji [Winter Solstice]   *KSZ* Vol.3 p.58
   Aka Fuji [Red Fuji]   *KSZ* Vol.3 p.59

6. 1970: *Taiyō wa Higashi kara Agaru* [The Sun Rises in the East]
   (Tokyo: Yayoi Shobō, 1970)
   Momo no Hi ni Momo no Hana   *KSZ* Vol.3 pp.116-7
      [On Peach Day Peach Blossoms]
   Fuyu no Asa no Sanpo [Winter Morning Walks]   *KSZ* Vol.3 pp.139-140
   Fuji   *KSZ* Vol.3 p.144
   Kakka Fuji [Volcano Fuji]   *KSZ* Vol.3 p.145

7. 1971: *Juraki no Hate no Sakkon* [These Days at the End of the Jurassic Period]
   (Tokyo: Yasaka Shobō, 1971)
   Fuji Ryū I-II [Dragon Fuji]   *KSZ* Vol.3 pp.181-182
   Unkai Fuji [Cloud Sea Fuji]   *KSZ* Vol.3 p.183

8. 1973: *Yonjū Hachinen Jiggu Zaggu no Shūi Shishū*
[1973 Zigzag Collection]
Fuji *KSZ* Vol.3 p.276

9. 1974: *Dekoboko* [Convex Concave]
(Tokyo: Chikuma Shobō, 1974)
Maboroshi no Fuji [Dream Fuji] *KSZ* Vol.3 p.358

10. 1975: *Zenten* [The Entire Firmament]
(Tokyo: Chikuma Shobō, 1975)
Chōchō San *KSZ* Vol.4 pp.39-40
Mangetsu Ryū [Full Moon Dragon] *KSZ* Vol.4 pp.68-9
Unjō Fuji [Fuji Above the Clouds] *KSZ* Vol.4 p.71
Kaijō Fuji [Sea Fuji] *KSZ* Vol.4 p.70
Fuji *KSZ* Vol.4 pp.72-3
Garasu no Tsuki [Glass Moon] *KSZ* Vol.4 p.73
Maboroshi no Fuji [Dream Fuji] *KSZ* Vol.4 pp.73-4

11. 1976: *Shokubutsu mo Dōbutsu* [Plants are Animals too]
(Tokyo: Chikuma Shobō, 1976)
Fuji San [Mt Fuji] *KSZ* Vol.4 p.156
Fuji Sono Isshun [Fuji Instant] *KSZ* Vol.4 pp.156-7
Yoru no Naka ni Shizumō to Suru Fuji *KSZ* Vol.4 pp.157-8
[Fuji about to Sink into the Night]

12. 1977: *Gen'on* [Fundamental Tone]
(Tokyo: Chikuma Shobō, 1977)
Fuji San [Mt Fuji] *KSZ* Vol.4 pp.199
Kuro Fuji [Black Fuji] *KSZ* Vol.4 pp.199-200
Enbō Fuji [A Distant View of Fuji] *KSZ* Vol.4 pp.227-8

13. 1979: *Ken'kon* [Heaven & Earth]
(Tokyo: Chikuma Shobō, 1979)
Maboroshi no Fuji [Dream Fuji] *KSZ* Vol.4 pp.238-9
Gotta ni no Utage [Mulligan Stew Feast] *KSZ* Vol.4 pp.270-1
Fuji San [Mt Fuji] *KSZ* Vol.4 p.313
Suigen Fuji [Fountainhead Fuji] *KSZ* Vol.4 p.314
Toyohata Shu [Mare's Tail Fuji] *KSZ* Vol.4 pp.316-7

14. 1980: *Unki* [Cloud Passage]
(Tokyo: Chikuma Shobō, 1980)
Daiōryū [Magnificent Dragon] p.4

15. 1981: *Gengen* [Pitch Pitch]
(Tokyo: Chikuma Shobō, 1981)
Kaichū Gensō [Undersea Fantasy] p.4
Fuji Gensō [Fuji Fantasy] p.12
Kiju no Fuji [Fuji at 77] p.62 ff.
Yuki o Kuu [Eating Snow] p.98
Nihon Rettō [Japanese Archipelago] p.142

16. 1982: *Genjō* [Mysterious Lute]
(Tokyo: Chikuma Shobō, 1982)
Ao Fuji [Blue Fuji] p.10

		Kaitei Fuji [Seabed Fuji]	p.14
		Genshi Fuji [Fuji Hallucination]	p.26
		Nisseki Fuji [Red Cross Fuji]	pp.106-8
17.	1983:	*Mirai* [The Future]	
		(Tokyo: Chikuma Shobō, 1983)	
		Daisōgyo [Giant China Carp]	pp.122-6
18.	1984:	*Genten* [Northern Firmament]	
		(Tokyo: Chikuma Shobō, 1984)	
		Fuji no Ishō [Fuji's Garments]	pp.4-6
		Fuji San [Mt Fuji]	p.8
		Sangatsu no Aru Asa no Fuji [Fuji on a Morning in March]	p.10
		Ihen [Extraordinary]	p.34
		Sōgyo to Ore no Tanjōbi [China Carp and My Birthday]	pp.62-6
19.	1985:	*Genkei* [Dreamscape]	
		(Tokyo: Chikuma Shobō, 1985)	
		Fuji Genkei [Fuji Dreamscape]	pp.4-5
		Fuji San [Mt Fuji]	pp.30-1
		1983.4 Nen no Waga Nyūyoku no Kiroku	pp.32-41
		[Record of My Baths 1983-4]	
		Fuji san [Mt Fuji]	p.58
20.	1986:	*Jimon Tamon* [Asking Myself/Asking Another]	
		(Tokyo: Chikuma Shobō, 1986)	
		Nisseki Fuji [Red Cross Fuji]	pp.2-7
		Naninani Fuji [Something Something Fuji]	pp.24-6
		Ore no Sanpo [My Walk]	pp.78-81

Leith Morton was born in Sydney in 1951 and read Japanese Literature at the University of Sydney, Dōshisha University and Kwansei Gakuin University. He is Senior Lecturer in Japanese at the University of Sydney. His other books include two volumes of poetry, a biography of the novelist Arishima Takeo entitled *Divided Self* and a volume of translations of modern Japanese fiction which he edited and co-translated.

Cid Corman (b.1924) is an American poet, editor of the internationally famed poetry journal *Origin*, who since 1958 has resided mostly in Kyōto. Author of over a hundred titles and translator of such poets as Francis Ponge, Paul Celan, Gottfried Benn, René Char and Eugenio Montale, Corman has with Kamaike Susumu translated Bashō's *Oku no Hosomichi* (Back Roads to Far Towns, 1968), many poems from the *Manyōshū* and three volumes of Kusano Shinpei's poetry.